LIONS

MELISSA GISH

PREDATORS X BOOKS

CREATIVE EDUCATION · CREATIVE PAPERBACKS

Published by Creative Education and Creative Paperbacks · P.O. Box 227, Mankato, Minnesota 56002 · Creative Education and Creative Paperbacks are imprints of The Creative Company · www.thecreativecompany.us · Design by Rita Marshall · Production by Christine Vanderbeek · Printed in the United States of America · Photographs by iStockphoto (Eric Isselée, kristian sekulic), Shutterstock (Baranov E, Thomas Barrat, boreala, panacea Doll, Fotogenix, grafixx, Eric Isselee, Stepan Kapl, Lychy, Stephen Marques, Graham Needham, Dikky Oesin, oorka, Susan Schmitz, Mogens Trolle, Riaan van den Berg, Vishnevskiy Vasily, Lara Zanarini)

Library of Congress Cataloging-in-Publication Data • Names: Gish, Melissa, author. • Title: Lions / Melissa Gish. • Series: X-Books: Predators. • Includes bibliographical references and index. • Summary: A countdown of five of the most dangerous lion encounters provides thrills as readers learn about the biological, social, and hunting characteristics of these grassland predators.

Identifiers: LCCN _ _ _ _
ISBN 978-1-60818-819-2 (hardcover) • ISBN 978-1-62832-422-8 (pbk) • ISBN 978-1-56660-867-1 (eBook)
Subjects: LCSH: TK—Juvenile literature. • Classification: LCC TK DDC TK—dc23

CCSS: TK RI.3.1, 2, 3, 4, 5, 7, 8, 10; RI.4.1, 2, 3, 4, 7, 10; RI.5.1, 2, 4, 10; RF.3.3, 4; RF.4.3, 4; RF.5.3, 4

First Edition HC 9 8 7 6 5 4 3 2 1 • First Edition PBK 9 8 7 6 5 4 3 2 1

LIONS

CONTENTS

PREDATORS X BOOKS

TIGERS
LIONS
JAGUARS
LEOPARDS

ROAR!

SCREAM!
HISS!
YOWL!

XCEPTIONAL FELINES

Lions are strong. Lions are fast. They have sharp teeth and claws. All other animals fear them. These big cats rule a vast kingdom. In Africa, lions are the grassland's most extreme predator.

Lion Basics

Lions are members of the cat family. Their closest relatives are tigers, leopards, and jaguars. Only these four cats can roar. Other cats yowl or scream. Lions roar the loudest of any cat.

Lions are **mammals**. Lions' golden fur helps them hide in dry grass. Lions have long tails with a dark tassel on the tip. Male lions have a mane of thick, dark fur around their neck. Female lions do not have a mane. Female lions are called lionesses.

AFRICAN LIONS

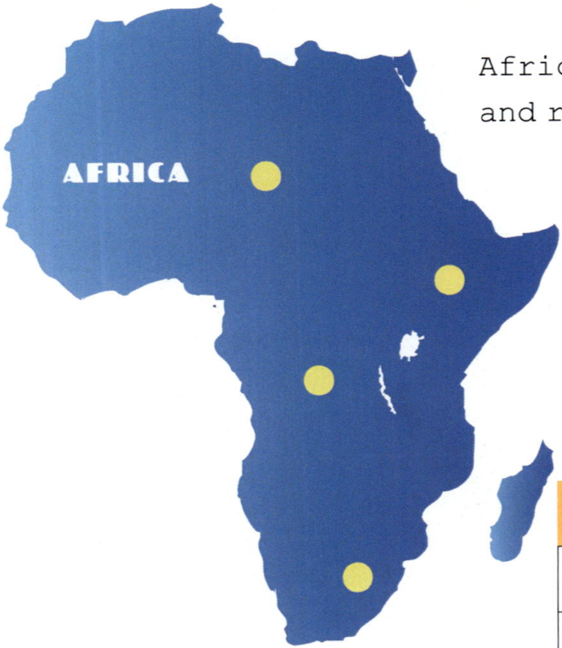

African lions live in various parks and reserves throughout Africa.

AFRICAN MALE LIONS

up to nine feet (2.7 m) long
about four feet (1.2 m) tall
about 400 pounds (181 kg)

AFRICAN LIONESSES

about nine feet (2.7 m) long
about four feet (1.2 m) tall
less than 300 pounds (136 kg)

LIONS' MANES

African male lions have bigger, thicker manes than Asiatic males.

ASIATIC LIONS

Asiatic lions are found only in India's Gir Forest National Park.

LIONS' TAILS

A lion's tail can be more than three feet (0.9 m) long.

ASIATIC MALE LIONS

- nearly 11 feet (3.4 m) long
- about four feet (1.2 m) tall
- up to 500 pounds (227 kg)

ASIATIC LIONESSES

- about nine feet (2.7 m) long
- about four feet (1.2 m) tall
- less than 300 pounds (136 kg)

Lions have four claws on each foot.
They are hidden in the toes.
The claws are attached to a bone
called a phalanx (*FAL-anks*).
It bends like a hinge.

Lions are carnivores. They eat meat. Animals killed by predators are called prey. Lions often hunt at night. Their eyes have a **reflective** coating that helps them see in dim light.

A lion's powerful jaws can crush bone. The four biggest teeth are canines. A lion's canine teeth can be up to four inches (10.2 cm) long. The scissor-like side teeth are carnassials. Lions have rough tongues that scrape meat from bone.

Carnivores survive by eating meat.

LIONS ARE CARNIVORES

LION BASICS FACT

A lion's claws are about one and a half inches (3.8 cm) long.

TOP FIVE XTREME LIONS

5

Xtreme Lion #5

Msoro Monty first appeared in the Luangwa River Valley in 1929. People began disappearing, and some were found torn to pieces. It had to be a lion. People tried to catch the man-eater, but the killing continued. Msoro Monty could smell a trap. He was never caught. Soon, he simply vanished. He may have died. No one knows what happened to Msoro Monty or exactly how many people he killed.

Lions do not normally hunt humans,

but about 70 people are killed by lions every year.

Lion Babies

Lion babies are called cubs. Lionesses usually have two to four cubs. Newborns weigh about two pounds (0.9 kg). They are blind and toothless. Their mother keeps them hidden. She feeds them milk from her body.

After about six weeks, she takes her cubs to her family group. Lion groups are called prides. All pride members help raise the cubs. Lionesses protect cubs from danger. Cubs chase their father's tail. This is the cubs' first hunting lesson.

Cubs also learn from older siblings. They all hunch down in the grass and creep forward. The young lions leap on each other and tussle in the grass. Playing helps cubs become powerful and skilled predators.

At about six months old, cubs no longer need their mother's milk. They share meals with the other lions. By one year of age, their teeth and claws are deadly sharp. They help the pride hunt prey.

at birth 2 pounds

Cubs are born

1 week

Open their eyes

3 weeks

Start to walk

litters of 4 cubs
6 weeks
8 weeks
1 year
2 years
4 years
Join the pride
Learn to hunt
Permanent teeth
Reproduce
6 months
180 pounds

LION BABIES FACT

Lions bond with members of their pride by rubbing faces and grooming each other. They even purr!

TOP FIVE XTREME LIONS

4

Xtreme Lion #4

Man-Eater of Mfuwe In 1991, this lion killed six people. It hunted in the Luangwa River Valley. Some victims were seized in the dark. Other times, the lion broke down doors to kill people in their homes. After one attack, the lion snatched up a laundry bag in its mouth and carried it through the village like a toy. Many people believed the lion was a demon. It was killed by Wayne Hosek.

XTRAORDINARY LIFESTYLE

Cats usually like to be alone. Lions are different from other cats. These extreme predators survive because they live and work together. A pride of lions is an unstoppable force.

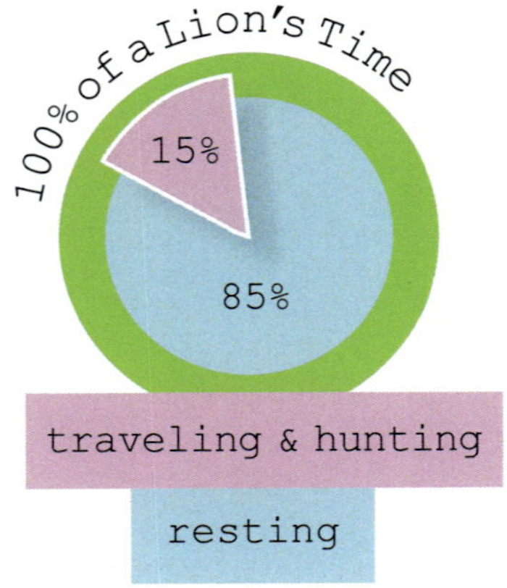

LION SOCIETY FACT

Lions spend about 20 hours a day resting and watching herds of animals.

LIONS LIVE IN PRIDES

Six to 40 members are in a pride.

Lion Society

In India, lions and lionesses live in separate prides. African prides include a male leader, his mates, daughters, and cubs, and sometimes one or two of his brothers. Male cubs are chased away when they grow up.

Each pride controls a **territory** with shade, water, and prey. Male lions with no territory wander alone or in small groups. Strong, young males may invade a territory. They challenge the leader for control.

Sometimes, the two males just stare at each other. The first to give up must go away. Other times, lions fight. Male lions may fight to the death to control a pride. A lion that takes over a pride kills all the cubs. He wants future cubs to be his alone.

XEMPLARY SKILLS

Although lionesses are the main hunters in a pride, they do not get to eat first. The pride leader eats first, then his brothers, and then the lionesses. The last to get food are the cubs.

XEMPLARY SKILLS FACT

The largest lions on Earth are found in Botswana's Okavango Delta. Cape buffalo and other large prey are abundant in this place.

In Africa, lions kill zebras, cape buffalo, wildebeest, and antelopes. Asiatic lions mostly hunt deer, antelopes, and water buffalo.

A hungry pride of lions is fearless. Lionesses work together to hunt. They can kill prey that weighs up to 1,000 pounds (454 kg). They watch for an animal to wander away from its herd. Then they spring into action.

Ambushing is one way lions hunt. They slowly sneak up on the animal. They get very close. Then, in a flash, one lioness leaps on the animal's back. She bites the spine. The animal stumbles. Another lioness bites the prey's throat. It cannot breathe. The other lionesses dig their claws into the animal's rump. They drag it to the ground.

TOP FIVE XTREME LIONS

Xtreme Lion #3

Lions of Tsavo From 1898 to 1899, two male lions killed dozens of workers building a railroad across the Tsavo River in Kenya. The lions dragged victims away at night. The workers nicknamed the lions "the Ghost" and "the Darkness." Reports said the lions killed 135 people. The lions actually killed only 35 people. The rest ran away from the railroad in fear. Big-game hunter Colonel John Henry Patterson killed the lions.

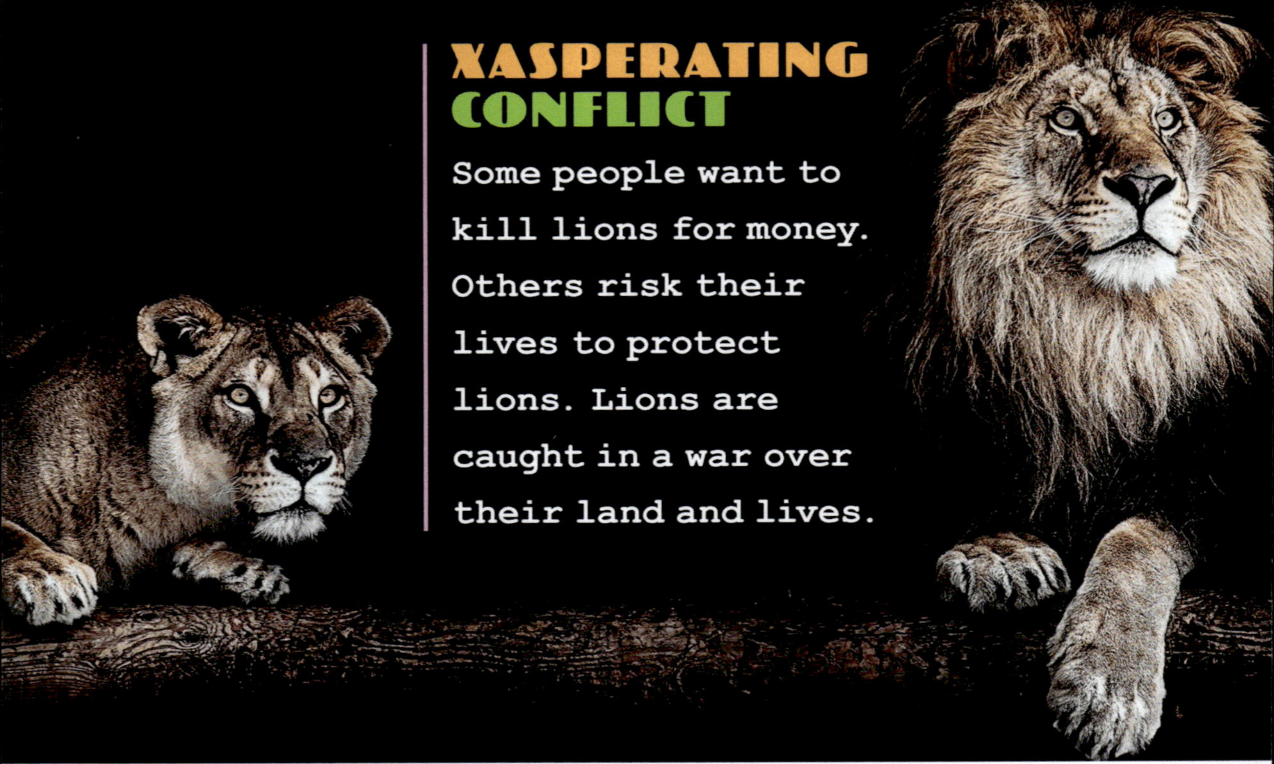

XASPERATING CONFLICT

Some people want to kill lions for money. Others risk their lives to protect lions. Lions are caught in a war over their land and lives.

Lion Survival

Adult lions have few natural enemies. Elephants may trample them. Packs of hyenas may attack sick or old lions. Humans are the lion's greatest threat. Killing lions is against the law. People who kill protected animals are called poachers. Usually, poachers shoot lions only for sport. They take the head and skin as **trophies**.

The number of people living in Africa is always growing. People need more land for farms and ranches. More than 80 percent of lions' habitat has been taken over by humans. People kill or drive away lions' prey. Lions must fight to survive on land shared with humans.

10,000 years ago	millions of lions
1960	500,000
Today	20,000
Tomorrow	?

Lions have learned that farm animals are easy meals. National parks and wildlife refuges are meant to be places where animals can live in the wild—without humans. In places like Tsavo and Kruger National Parks, lions are the top predators. Prey animals are abundant, so lion populations can be healthy. But even in protected places, Lions are not safe from poachers.

LION SURVIVAL FACT

Lions kill when they are hungry. If a pride has recently fed, prey around them will ignore the lions.

TOP FIVE XTREME LIONS

2

Xtreme Lion #2

Chiengi Charlie, the White Lion In 1909, this lion and two other male lions killed nearly 90 people. These man-eaters hunted in what is now Zambia. Chiengi Charlie was nicknamed "the White Lion" because his fur was nearly white. Charlie was clever. For years, he dodged bullets and traps. He was finally killed by a mail carrier named Galatea.

XCITING FACTS

Lions can go four to five days without drinking water.

Lions can run up to 50 miles (80.5 km) per hour for short distances.

The most successful prides are often those run by brothers.

Lion cubs have dark spots that make them hard to see among dry grass.

Each whisker on a lion's face has a black spot at its root.
Like human fingerprints, a lion's whisker spot pattern is unique.

Only about 2 in 10 lion cubs survive to see their second birthday.

A pride's territory can be as large as 100 square miles (259 sq km).

A male lion's roar can be heard almost five miles (8 km) away.

Lions have flabby bellies that protect their bodies from kicking prey animals.

Lions can leap up to 36 feet (11 m) with a running start.

Cubs practice their hunting skills by catching mice, lizards, and tortoises.

Lions do not chew their food—they swallow it whole!

Leo is a group of stars that looks like a crouching lion.
Leo gets its name from the Latin word for lion.

Male lions with the

darkest manes are healthier and stronger than other lions.

TOP FIVE XTREME LIONS

Xtreme Lion #1

Man-Eaters of Njombe A pride of 15 lions began killing people in southern Tanzania in 1932. To control disease in cattle, the government destroyed thousands of wildebeest, antelopes, and other animals. With little to eat, the lions turned to humans. They hunted in daylight and walked up to 20 miles (32.2 km) at night between villages. They eluded capture for 15 years, killing about 1,500 people.

GLOSSARY

mammals – animals with a backbone and fur or hair that feed their babies milk

offspring – the young of parents

reflective – able to throw back light like a mirror

territory – an area owned or claimed and defended from intruders

trophies – objects that are symbols of victory or success

RESOURCES

"All About Lions." Lion Research Center. University of Minnesota. http://cbs.umn.edu/research/labs/lionresearch/all-about-lions.

"Mammals: Lion." San Diego Zoo. http://animals.sandiegozoo.org/animals/lion.

Joubert, Dereck, and Beverly Joubert. *Face to Face with Lions*. Washington, D.C.: National Geographic, 2008.

Joubert, Dereck. *The Last Lions*. DVD. New York: National Geographic Entertainment, 2011.

INDEX

Male lions will sometimes form a group, called a coalition.